Photo by Michael Scott

The set from the Mint Theater Company production of "Uncle Bob." Set design by

UNCLE BOB

BY AUSTIN PENDLETON

★

DRAMATISTS
PLAY SERVICE
INC.

For George, Adam and Kelly

UNCLE BOB was produced by The Mint Theater Company (Kelly Morgan, Executive Artistic Director; Jonathan Bank, Producing Artistic Director), in New York City, on February 1, 1995. It was directed by Kelly Morgan; the set design was by Jeffrey Pajer; the costume design was by Paula Godsey; the lighting design was by Craig Caccamise; the dramaturg was Jennifer Wollerman; the sound design was by Carmen Borgia and the stage manager was Francys Olivia Burch. The cast was as follows:

BOB .... George Morfogen
JOSH .... Adam Sumner Stein

CHARACTERS

BOB, anywhere from his mid-forties to his early sixties.

JOSH, his nephew, anywhere from twenty to, say, twenty-seven. From the Midwest.

TIME

August. The present (1995).

PLACE

Bob's apartment in the West Village, in a brownstone, New York City.

UNCLE BOB should be performed without an intermission.

UNCLE BOB

SCENE 1

Bob sits writing at his desk, in a circle of light. It's night. The door to the apartment opens.

BOB.   All right, Sally, stop right there. *(Silence.)*

I mean, you don't have to be *silent,* I didn't say anything about being *silent,* but I don't think you better come into the room. Because you're going to start in, Sally, and I know, I know, I was a little sharp this morning, in fact, maybe it's better if you *don't* say anything because, I have to tell you, I don't like these fights. It's ruined the day, I haven't put down ten minutes on this thing — wait, let me turn it on — *(He turns on a tape recorder on the desk.)*

There, now maybe I can salvage this miserable day, maybe I — I knew you would turn up, you know, I've just been waiting. And of course that's taken up a lot of time, that's kept me from concentrating on my *thoughts* — look, Sally, I'm sorry for what I said this morning, even if it was *kind,* even if it was *pleasant,* because whatever it was it was *corrupt* because I didn't sleep last night, and you can say, "All right, I didn't know that, I thought eleven was late enough to call," well, Sally, have you ever heard of *night sweats? (Turns off tape recorder.)*

Well, I'm not going to record this, these are *complaints.* I mean, is that why you bought me this, so I could just record *complaints?* And you can play them at the memorial and everyone can say, "We're here to celebrate Bob's life" and everyone will realize that all they're celebrating is a bunch of *complaints?* I mean, Sally, I think you should examine why you bought me this. Do you want to *reveal* me, Sally? Sally, Sally, *give it up. (Silence.)*

I must say you're being very patient. Is this a strategy? Did you learn this somewhere, Sally? I suspect something, I have to lay it out, I suspect that you're in *group* or something. Since you moved out you've been different, you've been patient, you've been *dealing* with me, and forgive me, Sally, but I find that ridiculous. I mean, I think the whole idea of dealing with me is *romantic.* In the sentimental sense, not in the literary sense, not in the challenging sense. I mean, if you figure out how to deal with me, where is the *challenge,* and you always liked a challenge, Sally. I have to say I'm disappointed. I'm disappointed in you, Sally. I mean, I'm disappointed that you moved out, too, but that's different, I admire that, although I miss you. Sexually, I don't mean emotionally. All right I mean emotionally, too, I just don't mean *domestically.* Although I mean domestically, you said you would be by to *shop,* you haven't been for *two days.* Are you trying to show me that I'm *capable?* Again, you see, these things are *sentimental. (Silence.)*

This is working, you know. I feel a freedom, Sally. You see, that's the problem with you, I don't usually feel a *freedom* when we talk, and this is — if you could do this every couple of nights, just open the door and stand there and not *say* anything. *(Silence.)*

Could you do that, Sally? *(Silence.)*

Well, you see, now you've gone too far. You've ruined it. Sally, you are in many ways a remarkable person, I think you know I feel that, but you know, of course, you ruin things. I mean, you know that. You don't have to answer that, you don't have to *explain,* I mean for Christ's sake don't *defend* yourself, but if we can just — I'll sit here and you stand there — and if we can just *know* that together. That you invariably ruin — you see, the problem is that you're *corrupt,* Sally. But then — and I think this, by the way — women are corrupt. And I'm not saying that as a criticism, as a judgment, not necessarily, I mean I think we give too much significance to these words, and who knows, that corruption — this is an insight, Sally — that corruption women have may be the manifestation of a knowledge, of — and you notice I didn't call it an intuition, I mean I don't want you to be able to reduce my thinking to some — what do they call it, I resist these words they have now — *(Silence.)*

What do they call it? Jesus Christ. I can't *think*. Is that the illness? Or, no, no, maybe in this case it's my desire to avoid the word that will make my thought *generic*. I mean, is my mind disintegrating or is it just uncluttered? I mean, maybe that's all the dementia is, maybe I don't have to be afraid of it, maybe all it is is that you lose the next piece of garbage you were going to say, in fact maybe I'll *welcome* it because it will sweep out these *words* that are more and more being hurled into my mind as if it were a *dumpster* — I threw out the TV, by the way — and yes, I know, I *know*, it may sweep out other things as well, things even of value in my mind, but I tell you I'm beginning to think that will be a *small price* to pay. The word was chauvinism, by the way. I didn't use the word intuition because I didn't want you to think that what I said was chauvinist, not that you use those words, you don't hide behind those words, Sally, that's one of your best qualities, it's like your sexuality, if I may say so, it's *direct*. You're never *coy*, Sally. I always knew you wanted me, and I don't think I ever told you, that was a *help*. Anyway, this corruption, which let's face it is in all women, is just a manifestation of women's physical knowledge of the corruption that is at the heart of all organic processes, and that I, who sit here with my *mind*, am completely out of touch with, not that I don't have the superior perceptions. I mean, this is intricate terrain, Sally! And this silence you're maintaining, which started as a sound idea, so to speak, has now, I'm afraid, become as corrupt and enraging as you frequently become in conversation! I'm sorry, but I have to say it. *(Silence.)*

Now, why didn't I record *that*? That might have had some value. That might have provoked discussion at the memorial, and, Sally, if there's no discussion at my memorial, no, I mean vicious argument, I think it's going to be a waste of time. No, look, don't play anything. Because my remarks will just be misinterpreted and I won't be there to patiently, once again, set everybody straight. I'll tell you what. Play the tape, but just play silence. I mean a *reel* of silence, maybe with a coughing fit in the middle so they'll remember why they're there. But other than that, silence. Because, let's face it, I never say anything worth listening to, Sally. Well, there, you see that? This conversation with you has convinced me that nothing I say has any value, you see that, you have won again. What do you do, do you just sit around and think of ways to win? Because that's what I feel, whenever we talk, I feel defeated. And I don't even think of things I should have said because even when I do the next thing I think is what you would have said to *that.* Oh, Jesus. Stop provoking me, Sally. Will you just let *me* be silent for once, for Christ's sake? *(Silence.)*

Thank you. Thank you, sweetheart. *(Pause.)*

JOSH. *(Off.)* Holy shit. *(Pause.)*

BOB. What?

JOSH. Uncle Bob, that is like *troubled.*

BOB. Josh?

JOSH. *(Enters.)* It's Josh, yeah, but Uncle Bob —

BOB. What do you think you're doing? You just walk into somebody's apartment — this is New York! —

JOSH. Hey! The door was open!

BOB. The door was unlocked! The door was not *open,* it was —

JOSH. Uncle Bob, if the door is unlocked, I mean today, I mean like in this fucking jungle that you live in, Uncle Bob, then that's the same as if the door was *open* —

BOB. No, it's not the same as if it's open. When a door is open, Josh, it's *ajar,* it's in a different physical position than when it's closed. And this door was closed. And there is no way from the outside to know if it is locked or unlocked. I mean, *I* know. *I* know it's unlocked, and that gives me pleasure, Josh, to have that secret knowledge, but you did not know it was unlocked, and that can only mean you *turned the knob* —

JOSH. Oh, fuck.

BOB. You can say "oh fuck" all you want but that does not change the fact you *turned the knob.* How can I make you see

10

that? That's always been your problem, no one can make you see the simplest things, I can't, your father can't — *(Josh starts to speak.)* Let me finish! You never let me finish! Your father says that's how you get into the trouble that you do, you just presume, you never ask, just like you obviously got on the Greyhound and came all the way here, without calling, after months, *months* of silence, of evident disinterest about the fact that your Aunt Sally and I were still *alive,* you just *came,* without asking if you —

JOSH.   Uncle, Bob, I turned the knob. You know? That's all I did. I don't know what came over me, but, you know? I turned the knob. I mean, I don't even think that's *subconscious,* Uncle Bob. I don't think your argument *holds up.* I mean, I *turned the knob.* Look, what do you think I should have done? I mean, I'd like to know! —

BOB.   Knocked. Knocked, Josh. That's what I would have liked —

JOSH.   Well, see, I didn't want to *do* that.

BOB.   Why not? You see? That's what I mean! That's what your father says, we've talked about this, by the way! —

JOSH.   Will you just leave him out of this? I mean, what *is* this? He says that's what my *problem* is? My *problem* is if I don't want to do something I don't *do* it? I mean, is that a *problem* according to my Dad? Well, yes, I guess it is! —

BOB.   Josh, Josh, you see? Now I'm angry. You see that? You will not listen to the simplest, the most *loving criticism.* You are a *disaster,* Josh. And you're not a worthless person, by the way —

JOSH.   Aw, man —

BOB.   Well, you're not! And I say that to no one! Sally occasionally. But all I'm saying is, all your father and I are saying is when you go to someone's house — uninvited, Josh! — you knock on the door. You don't *turn the knob.* And —

JOSH.   Hey. Uncle Bob. Focus. Focus, Uncle Bob. What if I knocked on the door and you said, "Who's there?" Did you think of that?

BOB.   I thought of that. I thought I'd say, "Who's there?" I mean, I'm not sure I specifically articulated it in my *mind,* but —

JOSH. Yeah, but, Uncle Bob, then what? Then what? See, you're like Dad, you say things, but you don't think through what will actually *happen* —

BOB. What will happen is you'll say, "It's Josh."

JOSH. That's right. Good, Uncle Bob. Good. I'll say, "It's Josh," because I don't *conceal* these things. But then what?

BOB. I'll say, "Come in." Look, I'm *tired.* I'm ill, for Christ's sake!

JOSH. Yeah, but stay with me for a minute here. You'll say, "Come in." I mean, you *say* you'll say "come in" but I don't think so. I think you'll say — and I don't want to like put words into your mouth — but I think you'll say, "Josh, for Christ's sake, what do *you* want? What are you *doing* here?" And then we'll like get into this *discussion,* and I won't come up with the right *answer,* and before you know it I'll be on the way back home, without even getting in the *door* —

BOB. All this is possible.

JOSH. Well, there you go. And all I'm saying is, that is why I didn't knock, to prevent that stupid conversation from like *taking place,* and the only other option open to me was to *turn the knob,* and like I say I didn't think, it's just something that I did, and, Uncle Bob, I have to say I think it's *sick* that it was actually open. But, look, that's yours, hey, that's yours, Uncle Bob, and, look, I'm sorry if I scared you. I didn't mean —

BOB. You didn't scare me!

JOSH. Of course I scared you!

BOB. Don't tell me I am scared when I am not scared! That's an invasion of my privacy! You see that, you just walk in and *presume* —

JOSH. You were scared, Bob! I said, "Holy shit," and —

BOB. Just get back on that bus!

JOSH. No, I'm not getting on the fucking bus! I'm telling you that you were scared, and if you'll *listen* to me I'm telling you you have no reason to be scared because, I don't care, a killer could walk in here, Riker's fucking *Island* could walk in here and all he'd have to do is listen to that sick rap with Aunt Sally and believe me, Uncle Bob, they wouldn't take another *step*. I mean they'd be like *paralyzed*. I mean, that's better than like fucking *Mace!* —

BOB.   And that's another thing.

JOSH.   What?

BOB.   You just walk into somebody's house and every other word is *fucking*, for Christ's sake. I mean, the word, the use of the word, means nothing to me, what enrages me is that *it's my home* —

JOSH.   Look, I don't mean to like *offend* you. Pardon me if I *offend* you.

BOB.   You don't offend me! You bore me! You have always bored me, in that way that people who might otherwise be worth something bore me. I can't stand it! It's like their unrealized potential is just sitting there, sucking up the oxygen! —

JOSH.   OK, OK, I *bore* you! Is that a *crime?* And stop telling me I'm worth something or I'm not worth something, I mean, what are you, the fucking *Treasury?* And also *you* like to say, "for Christ's sake" all the time. So "for Christ's sake" is OK but "fucking" is not OK, is that right? Is that *it,* I mean? I mean, *I* don't like "for Christ's sake," *I* don't like this "Jesus" shit you keep saying, I mean, that offends me, so just suck on *that,* but, look, I'll put up with it! —

BOB.   You see, the worst part of this is that I'll have to call your father. I mean, I'm sure he doesn't know where you are, which may, although he won't admit it, be a relief to him, but —

JOSH.   *(Overlap.)* Uncle Bob, Uncle Bob — look, I like you, Uncle Bob, and it is great to see you, but you know? You call my Dad I'm going to beat the shit out of you —

BOB.   Josh, physical threats don't mean anything to me anymore. Physical threats have lost their *charm.*

JOSH.   Oh, come on, you think I *mean* that? I didn't *mean* that! —

BOB.   I don't care what you mean and what you don't mean! I just want you to get on the bus and go back —

JOSH.   Will you stop *assuming* I took the fucking bus? I did not take the fucking bus!

BOB. I don't care how you got here, Josh!

JOSH. Well, good! Good! Then stop *assuming* that I —

BOB. Oh, for Christ's sake.

JOSH. What? —

BOB. Oh, no. Oh, no. Did you hitch?

JOSH. Yes, I *hitched.* Big *deal.*

BOB. Well, now I'm very angry.

JOSH. Well, I'm *sorry.* OK, you're *angry* now. Boy, Uncle Bob, these *mood swings* are just *terrifying!* —

BOB. If anything had happened to you I'd have been responsible, but then of course do *you* care? —

JOSH. Oh. Oh, I get it. You'd have been *responsible* —

BOB. That's right —

JOSH. So then you like have *trouble* with that —

BOB. Yes, I have trouble with that. What if I'd gotten a — *phone call* from your father, or, even worse, your mother, saying you'd been found dead. You see, your father would say, *stoically,* "Bob, don't blame this on yourself. Josh loved you, that's why he was on the way to see you," but your mother would say, "Bob, I think we've got to *work through our feelings,*" that's what she always used to say to Sally, "Bob has got to work through his feelings," 'til Sally told her, *brilliantly,* "Don't worry, Bob has no feelings to work through." "What you see is what you get," she told her. And your mother, poor, dear, driven spirit that she is, was *stopped* —

JOSH. Wait. See, I don't know how to *answer* this —

BOB. Well, you don't have to. You don't have to answer everything —

JOSH. I mean, I don't know where to *start* with this. I mean, I'm dead, right? I'm probably slashed to ribbons right there on Route 80. But I mean the *issue* is, which is the better *phone conversation,* if you hear it from my mother or my father —

BOB. Josh, each minute — each minute that you're here makes me happier that I am dying. And I don't mean that as an insult, Josh. What I mean is you will find that when that happens to you —

JOSH. It's already happened to me, Uncle Bob! I'm dead! But that's no hassle at all, it looks like, next to the hassle that my mom is going to say, "Work through your feelings, Bob!" —

BOB. Will you shut up? What you'll find, Josh, is that time is *precious.* Do you hear that? Time is precious. Now, you may not have known that you were visiting a dying man but if you did I'm sure you're disappointed that you came across Route 80 to hear the wisdom of the dying and that the wisdom of the dying is *banalities.* Banalities! I know *I'm* disappointed. The thoughts that crowd me when I'm trying to sleep, the consolations that I come to after hours of *weeping* in the dark, are insights I would have called calendar poetry when I was well. And, Josh, this is an insight, that is why we hate clichés so much, not out of literary scruple like I thought, no, it's because we know somehow that clichés are what are going to come to us when we are dying! —

JOSH. OK, O*K!* —

BOB. Don't say "OK, OK" to me! Don't *ever* say "OK, OK" to me! I'm telling you something. I'm telling you that time is precious, time is as precious as that *plate,* that heirloom, which is the only precious thing in this apartment other than the time that you are *wasting,* Josh, which is why I'm so happy I am dying, because when I am dead I will not have to sit here and watch everybody *waste time,* as you have wasted all the time that you've been given in your life —

JOSH. Look —

BOB. — wasted the college education your grandmother gave you —

JOSH. Look, just leave her out of —

BOB. — wasted, *totalled,* the four cars your parents bought for you, and, most important, wasted every conversation I or I'm sure anybody else has put aside their time, their intellectual reserve, their passion, even their sexual passion, to try to have with you —

JOSH. Look, Uncle Bob — *(Smashes plate, goes right on.)* Look, Uncle Bob, *please.* Whoa, Bob. Look, look, we've gotten off the *track* here. I mean, all I said — all I *meant* to say — was look at what you're saying, Bob! About me, and I'm dead, and the phone call and my mom and dad, and I was just say-

15

ing look at it. And then you like freak out and say that time is precious, and, look, I know time is precious, Bob. You don't *know* how precious time is until you waste it, Bob. So just, I mean, whoa! And furthermore, Bob, furthermore I didn't even get a chance to tell you the other thing that, what, got to me, that freaked *me* out — no, freaked me out is going too far — I'm sorry about the plate, I really am, but, Bob, you *know?* — but anyway the second thing you said about my like being dead was, you *assumed,* Bob, you *presumed* that Mom and Dad would know that I was coming to see *you.* As if like East was Uncle Bob. But, Bob, the Eastern United States is a *big thing.* Would you like to see an Atlas, Bob? Because I have one in my bag —

BOB.   I don't want to see an Atlas.

JOSH.   OK, OK, that's cool. And if you change your mind that's cool, too, but anyway — look, I am *bummed out* about that plate — anyway, I could have been heading for *Vermont,* it's not like every time I *set out* it's to see *you,* I mean, I *like* you, Bob —

BOB.   When have you ever come East except to see me? Except to hang around here and make Aunt Sally shop for you, and disappear for nights at a time and leave us to make excuses when your parents called, and make us take you to see *sights* that *bored* you from the moment that we paid admission? When, Josh? Except for that school trip, which frankly I resented because —

JOSH.   Oh. So you resented my *school trip.* Boy, see, Bob, you save your anger for the *big things* —

BOB.   — because you asked me to come up and meet you and your classmates and your *teacher* at Sardi's, and I had to sit there and eat *chicken* while nobody had a clue of what to say to me because I was your loser uncle who had fled to New York, and Sally wasn't there to talk to them —

JOSH.   Aunt Sally was working for the *homeless,* Bob.

BOB.   That's right. Aunt Sally was working for the homeless.

JOSH.   Well, see, is that my fault? Look, I'm hot, you know? I'm sweaty —

BOB.   I don't care. I don't care, Josh. And your teacher said,

16

so they could *hear*, said, "Didn't you work for your brother back at home, sir?" And I said, "Yes." That's all I said. I thought, "Lady, this is up to you." I said, "Yes," and that is all I said.

JOSH. See, that's it, you never talk when anybody's *there*.

BOB. What are you saying? That is untrue! I've been talking to you since you walked in here! —

JOSH. Yeah, but you've been carrying on to me like you were carrying on to Aunt Sally, and Aunt Sally wasn't even here! —

BOB. Will you let me finish? So then there was this *pause*. Which lasted until *coffee*. And then your teacher said, "Oh, I remember you." And I thought maybe I had *slept* with her or something. I mean, she was an English teacher. But, no, what she remembered was when I played the lead in *Harvey* with your mother's *group*. She said, "You know, I've never seen anybody give that interpretation to that part," as if it were Hamlet, or King Lear, or, or Oedipus, for Christ's sake! And I said, "Ah," that's all I said, because what was I to say? Was I to tell her that I'd tried to emphasize the *alcoholism* of the character, the alcoholic despair of the oldest son of a local family that had once been great, but whose oldest son was now best friends with a rabbit? A rabbit that no one else could see? And that I knew from working on the role that this man was in love with this rabbit, and I mean sexually, desperately, Josh, I mean this man was desolate when this rabbit didn't *call*. Could I tell her that? Because that was how I played the part, and, Josh, that production was a *flop*. *Harvey* was a flop. And your mother, your poor mother, who put that play on just for me, because she knew I wasn't happy working for your father, because she knew I had a spiritual crisis every time I saw an *invoice*, and she thought I needed to express myself because she knew I had played Hamlet back in college — well, all your mother did was antagonize the whole community. She wanted to bring me together with the community, and all she got was a revisionist *Harvey* that lost her several friends, I think. I said to Sally, we're leaving here, it hasn't worked, that's all. And then you follow me, time after time, relentlessly, and finally with your *teacher*, and I'm on display, at *Sardi's*, as if I were going to a *musical* or something — the loser uncle! I tell you, I've had an easier time with AIDS than with being designated as the loser uncle, I mean there is more *hope* in having AIDS, at least I know they're *working* on it, at least I know that you can get a *catheter* —

JOSH.   See, you keep bringing that up —

BOB.   What? What do I bring up?

JOSH.   That you're sick. That you're like dying. You keep *working it in* to the conversation —

BOB.   Well, forgive me, Josh. I don't mean to be *coy*. I don't mean to be asking for your *sympathy* —

JOSH.   It's not that! I mean, I know you have AIDS. I mean, everybody *knows* it —

BOB.   Oh, they do.

JOSH.   It's the talk of the fucking *town*, Bob. I mean, they're so *relieved*. Not that they want you to die, don't *freak*, I mean relieved because now they can like *figure you out* —

BOB.   Oh, I see! I have AIDS, so they can figure me out!

JOSH.   Well, yeah.

BOB.   I resent that!

JOSH.   Well, there you go *again*.

BOB.   They have figured me out!

JOSH.   Bob, it's no big *deal!* People like to figure things out! —

BOB.   And that's why this epidemic has developed!

JOSH.   *What?* What are you *talking* about?

BOB.   This illness has developed in the vicious, unrelenting war against privacy! This virus developed because *People* magazine was not *enough*, even the *National Enquirer* was finally *discreet*, so —

JOSH.   Oh, come on, Bob! You think too much, did anybody ever tell you —

BOB.   This virus has been sent so that I could be figured out, which I have spent my life avoiding, to — to *scrambling* —

JOSH.   Bob, this virus has been sent because somebody fucked a monkey! And you got it because you took it up the ass! OK, OK, rough shake of the dice, Bob, but *People* magazine, give me a *break*. And anyway that's why I'm here, I thought you'd maybe need some help. I thought, OK, he took it up the ass in like an epidemic, that's really like *intelligent*, but at least he can't talk to me about *smoking* anymore. I mean, the fucker probably needs a helping hand to stick him with an *IV* or something —

BOB.   So this — this is a visit of *compassion?* —

JOSH.   Look! Don't get smart! OK? Don't get *witty!*

BOB.   I'm not being witty! I am never witty! I'm saying, did you come here to be my *buddy?*

JOSH.   Your buddy? I'm not your *buddy,* Uncle Bob.

BOB.   No, that's a term. It's a term. You don't know what a buddy is? You're living in the past, Josh! A buddy is someone they *send* to someone who has —

JOSH.   Oh. Is this a *gay* thing?

BOB.   No. Well, yes. I mean, the concept started with a gay organization —

JOSH.   I'll bet.

BOB.   Look, would you just like to leave?

JOSH.   No, Bob, I'm not *leaving.*

BOB.   So I'm about to die of AIDS, attended by my homophobic college dropout nephew —

JOSH.   Bob, why does this sofa not pull out? The other times it *pulled out.* I mean, what the fuck is this?

BOB.   I threw that sofa out when your Aunt Sally left. And if you don't like it, as I say, you can just —

JOSH.   Wait. Aunt Sally has moved out?

BOB.   Oh, come on, Josh. Sally moved out three months ago. You didn't *know* that?

JOSH.   No! I —

BOB.   What is the matter with this family? This family used to be a network! —

JOSH.   Hey! Don't just like *assume* that Mom and Dad don't know it. Hey, Bob, I'm sure they talk about it *all the time.* I just don't *listen,* OK? I mean, I tune out when they talk about you. I mean, your life *depresses* me —

BOB.   Josh, you know, there is a deeper problem here.

JOSH.   Well, I hope so. I *really* hope so.

BOB.   The problem is, you stood in that doorway and you heard me tell Sally that I missed her. Now, are you so far gone, so self-absorbed —

JOSH.   Bob, Bob, let me tell you something. I wasn't listening to the *words*, Bob, I was like *zoning* on the fact that you were talking for twenty minutes to a fucking *door* and calling it Aunt Sally. I wasn't like taking in every little *turn of phrase* that you —

BOB.   Turn of phrase? I said, "Since you moved out, Sally." I think I said it *twice*. Well, I don't know exactly, but, look, I have it here on tape, I'll *play* it —

JOSH.   Bob! Don't play it! I don't want to hear it again, Bob! Besides, you turned it off, you said these were *complaints,* and then you turned it off. And then you went on talking to Aunt Sally and, I tell you, Bob, the *world went away.* OK? OK? Now, look, you threw out the guest sofa after Sally left, OK, I get it, that's a *signal,* but, Bob, do you have *sheets?* That's all I want to know! Sheets!

BOB.   Why are you *here!* This is a nightmare!

JOSH.   I'm here because you have the Big One! What is there to under*stand?* I'm going to look for sheets, Bob. *(He disappears.)*

BOB.   Let me tell you something, Josh. When a person has AIDS a certain — what am I going to call it? — pessimism comes along with it. And pessimism is something that can only really be enjoyed in private. I've tried it in public but it's a *hard sell,* people get upset, that's what Aunt Sally and I fought about this morning, she made me go to a *healing circle* last night, I mean I fought it! But you know Aunt Sally, she would not let up, and so I went, and finally I couldn't take it anymore, I said to them, "Why are we holding hands, for Christ's sake! We're about to die!" And I left! And then when Sally called this morning, to *check up* on it, and I told her what I said, well, she got very, very angry, but, anyway, you see my point.

JOSH.   *(Off.)* I can't say that I do, Bob.

BOB.   My point is that one of the luxuries of this disease is that you get to cry out in despair in the middle of the night and it doesn't feel indulgent. It doesn't feel *literary* like it used to, it doesn't seem like a yearning for the nineteenth century. *(Josh reappears dressed for bed.)* And if you insist on sleeping here — and I have to say this, it's rude to come into someone's house and put on your pajamas — but, all right, you've done it, but if I feel a twinge of self-consciousness the next time I cry out in the middle of the night, if you take that away from me, forget the plate, Josh, *forget the plate, then* I will be very angry. You are on probation is what I'm trying to say —

JOSH.   Hey, look, I'm tired. And, you know, there are no sheets. Except on your bed, and *no way* am I going to take those. Hey, goodnight, OK? *(Has spread a blanket; lies down.)*

BOB.   When your aunt left I offered those sheets — the guest sheets — to the woman across the hall. Three small children, I thought, she could *use* them. She looked at me as if I were offering her something — something — *(He stops. Pause.)* I offered to wash them, downstairs, on the hot cycle, and she could watch. She said no, and thanked me, and closed the door and I burned them in the hallway.

JOSH.   *(Sleepy.)* What a guy.

BOB.   Well, I see I've *bored* you. I'm going to say one thing for myself, Josh. I'm going to make one claim for my whole life. I am not bored.

JOSH.   Hey, I need my sleep, Bob. Go in the other room and cry out in despair or some — fucking thing — will you?...

BOB.   I *will*, Josh. Just be *patient*. *(Silence.)* Josh? *(Josh mumbles.)* This isn't fair, Josh, I am wound up. I'm on a roll. *(Josh sleeps.)* Oh, well. What do you *expect*? *(Josh sleeps. Bob watches. Lights.)*

SCENE 2

Bob is sitting at the window. Josh enters from the rain, with groceries. It's late afternoon; early evening the next day. Nothing has changed in the apartment.

JOSH.   Aw, man.

BOB.   Good evening, Josh.

JOSH.   Good evening?! What do you *mean?* Are you saying good evening because it's *raining?* I mean, I'm sure that *turns you on! — (Puts bag down; goes into the other room.)*

BOB.   I mean good evening, Josh. It's a *phrase.* And I don't get to say good evening to anybody anymore.

JOSH.   *(Off.)* Well, Bob, there's a reason for that.

BOB.   Shut up, Josh. I'm in a *good mood.*

JOSH.   *(Off.)* When did this happen? Did this happen while I was at D'Agostino's?

BOB.   Yes. I sat here thinking. I was going to write but instead I thought.

JOSH.   *(Re-enters in a clean T-shirt; starts unpacking groceries.)* What did you think about, Bob?

BOB.   I don't know. I thought about so many things. I thought about the fact that I had looked forward, Josh, to dying alone. I had looked forward to the clarity of being in agony and *unattended.* But you, of course, have ruined that, and so I had to *think things through,* and I thought, well, if I died alone, I might actually end up thinking my endurance was heroic, and *that* would be a stupid way to go. I don't want to die *fatuously,* Josh. And then, of course, if you weren't here, the chances are I wouldn't be allowed to die alone, I mean Sally would be here, and your mother, and your father, and it's possible that that would lead me to a last-minute acceptance of the idea that people can actually be of use to one another, and, Josh, that *weighs in* against everything I know. I don't mean people are bad — those people I mentioned are *good,* Josh — I mean that people are of no use to one another. I have fought for that idea against sometimes nearly unconquerable odds because I seem to attract good people in my life, but I have fought for it because it squares with what we've come to in this world. It squares with the removal of all things that exist only to be *nice,* and I am not afraid of that development, I face it, I face the time I live in, Josh, and I will die facing it because that is the meaning of this epidemic, the meaning of this epidemic is to crystallize the fact that no one can do anything for anybody anymore —

JOSH.   I thought the meaning of this thing was *People* magazine, Bob —

BOB.   Wait, I'm not —

JOSH.   Make up your *mind,* Bob.

BOB.   Will you let me finish? I'm saying the times are trash! And, Josh, in you the trashy horror of the times — and I don't mean this as an insult — is vividly alive to me. There is a purity about the way that you reflect what we have come to. You are the holy fool of garbage, Josh, the —

JOSH.   SHIT! SHIT! SHIT!

BOB.   And I must ask you not to interrupt me!

JOSH.   They didn't pack the milk. They didn't bag the milk. Now I have to go *back* there, in the *rain* —

BOB.   Well, why didn't you notice it then? You never *notice* anything —

JOSH.   Bob, this is not my fault. Time out, Bob. This is not mine.

BOB.   No, Josh, being around you all these years, watching you, has been like standing on the bank of a river watching a barrel which may have things of value in it drift away on some mysterious current —

JOSH.   And they forgot to bag the juice. Those *faggots.*

BOB.   Josh, those are fine, courteous young Hispanic women. Give me the receipt.

JOSH.   Why?

BOB.   Josh, you didn't *buy* the milk. You didn't *buy* the juice.

JOSH.   I bought the milk, Bob, I remember buying the —

BOB.   No, Josh, you remember *looking* at the milk. You remember *looking* at the juice. Look at the receipt, Josh. Nowhere does it say —

JOSH.   Of course it doesn't say it! They didn't ring it up! And they didn't ring it up because they didn't bag it! I worked at a supermarket, Bob, I *know* these things, I've *done* this —

BOB.   How long did you work at the supermarket, Josh? How long did *that* job last?

JOSH.   Look, *you* go back there. *You* go back in the rain —

BOB.   The point is not who goes back in the rain —

JOSH.   Yes, it is! That's the point, Bob! The point is not talking about *me* all the time! The point is not how long I held down some job at the *Giant,* the point is not about me, ever! The point is — face it! — who goes back there in the rain!

BOB.   Why did you not consult the list I gave you?

JOSH.   I threw away the list. I don't like lists.

BOB.   Then how are we supposed to get our groceries?

JOSH.   A few at a time. OK? Is that *OK?* —

BOB.   No, no, it is not OK. I mean, for *my* sake it's OK —

JOSH.   But not mine. Are you trying to straighten me out, Bob? Or, no.

BOB.   Well, yes.

JOSH.   No, let me rephrase the question. Are *you,* Bob — are *you* trying to straighten me out?

BOB.   Well —

JOSH.   This is not fair. This is not fair. You *too,* Bob? *You?* —

BOB.   Josh, calm down! Hear me out! I'm trying to straighten you out because I know that I will fail! And that exhilarates me. Because — and this is the point I was heading toward before you interrupted me —

JOSH.   You were heading toward a *point?*

BOB.   Yes, and that point is I am dying —

JOSH.   I know that! Will you *stop?*

BOB.   — and I am terrified that the fact that I am dying will make me *sentimental,* will frighten me into coming up with some *meaning* to my life, but if I try to straighten you out, if I put effort into giving you a sense of purpose, of a future, not only will I fail, which will be thrill enough, I will be *up against it,* up against the fact that there is no future that can possibly mean anything to you. And I will die not hanging on to any hope, and the meaninglessness of my death will leap up into a harmony with the meaninglessness of your life, and I will know a peace, the peace that I have always longed for, Josh. So thank you. Thank you for coming here. And that's what I was thinking while you went to D'Agostino's. *(Pause.)*

JOSH.   Well, I don't know what to *say.*

BOB.   You don't have to say anything. I'm tired.

JOSH.   Don't say you're tired. I mean, you can't just dump that shit and say you're tired. I bought a candy bar.

BOB.   A candy bar?

JOSH.   For you. I thought you might want something *bad.*

BOB.   Why, thank you, Josh.

JOSH.   I mean, what am I supposed to *do* here? Just hang out and be stupid? And then you'll try to make me not be stupid, but I'll keep on being stupid, and then you'll like find God or something? I mean, I want to make sure I have this *right* —

BOB.   Change your T-shirt.

JOSH.   What?

BOB.   Your T-shirt.

JOSH.   I just changed it, Bob, *didn't you notice?*

BOB.   But you didn't dry yourself.

JOSH.   Why should I dry myself?

BOB.   So that you won't be wet, Josh. So you won't catch a cold.

JOSH.   Bob, are you giving health tips now? Because I'll give it to you straight —

BOB.   Will you please change your shirt?

JOSH.   No, I won't change my shirt.

BOB.   Well, then, I'm going to bed.

JOSH.   What?

BOB.   I'm going into my room, and I am going to shut the door, and I am going to read some *Hemingway,* unless you go into the closet, and you get a T-shirt, and you go into the bathroom and you *shut the door,* and *dry* yourself —

JOSH.   OK, *OK* —

BOB. I mean, I don't know why you're doing this! Is this your self-destructiveness, or are you showing off, or is it some ecstatic combination of the two —

JOSH. Hey! Bob! I'll change the shirt! Just shut up, Bob, and let me *change the shirt! (He storms off. Bob picks up a book, reads. Josh enters.)* How's this? Is this OK? Aw, man —

BOB. What?

JOSH. You're *reading.*

BOB. Yes.

JOSH. You said if I changed my shirt you wouldn't read. Hey! This is our time! *(Grabs book, throws it in the wastebasket.)*

BOB. All right.

JOSH. All right what?

BOB. You say this is our time. Use it.

JOSH. Hey! I feel like on the spot!

BOB. Well, when you go and visit somebody who's dying you *are* on the spot. Particularly if you *move in.*

JOSH. And, see, I don't believe you.

BOB. What don't you believe?

JOSH. I don't believe a word you said, Bob. I think you want to die happy, which is cool! —

BOB. Josh —

JOSH. See, Bob, there is a problem here.

BOB. I'm sure there is.

JOSH. Bob, what if I come out with something that like cheers you up? What if I say something with some smarts in it, or, shit, Bob, you know, *hope?* I mean, chill, I don't really know what that would *be,* but, Bob, you never *know.* Then what? Have I failed? I mean, I want to know! —

BOB. I think I'll go back to Hemingway — *(Reaches for wastebasket.)*

JOSH. Stay out of that wastebasket.

BOB. Josh, you're going to have to do better than this —

JOSH. I mean, Hemingway *shot* himself. And *he's* the one you're going to listen to? Listen to *me!*

BOB. Well, there are so many ways to answer that that I don't think I'll answer it at *all* —

JOSH. Because I'll tell you something. Your death is not

meaningless. Your death is awesomely *stupid*, Bob, which is the opposite of meaningless because the stupidity is *all yours*. You are the captain of your *soul*, Bob. Oh, right, you're *reading*. Well, Bob, all I am saying is you took it up the ass right in the middle of an epidemic, which I don't get because you had Aunt Sally *right* —

BOB.   Wait a minute.

JOSH.   Wait a minute what?

BOB.   What's Sally got to do with this?

JOSH.   Well, that's the big one, Bob. That's what everybody wants to know.

BOB.   Sally has nothing to do with what has happened to me!

JOSH.   Well, some people think that's like the problem. And I don't get, I, for one, I think Aunt Sally's *hot* —

BOB.   Oh, for Christ's sake!

JOSH.   Stop saying that!

BOB.   I'll say anything I want! And I'll permit no one to imply that Sally failed me just because I — just because —

JOSH.   Because what? Say it, Bob!

BOB.   Oh, well, I see. I see what you're up to.

JOSH.   What? I don't —

BOB.   I never thought that you were cheap, Josh. Trashy, but not cheap. I really never thought that you were cheap.

JOSH.   What cheap? What did I say? —

BOB.   You want a description of the behavior that infected me.

JOSH.   What?

BOB.   I challenge you to talk to me and all you can come up with is a clumsy probe into the sexual details —

JOSH.   Bob, I am not *interested* —

BOB.   That's why you came to see me!

JOSH.   Bob, look, I don't care that it was homosexual behavior. I've got nothing *against* homosexual behavior. I mean, I think it's disgusting, and when I think of it I dry-heave, but, Bob, you know me.

BOB.   Josh —

JOSH.   I am into happiness, Bob.

27

BOB.   Josh, try to grasp this. I am not a homosexual.

JOSH.   Well, Bob, tell it to the judge.

BOB.   Is that what you think, then? You think —

JOSH.   Bob, what I generally do is, I work with the evidence. And, Bob, unless you're into drugs, which I don't think you are, and I applaud that, Bob! —

BOB.   Josh, I'm not denying I hit the street. I'm not denying I took it up the ass, if that's the phrase we've settled on —

JOSH.   I think it works, Bob, I really think —

BOB.   Well, good, then, that's the one we'll use. But does this mean I'm gay, Josh? Does this *in itself* —

JOSH.   OK, we'll go for bi. Let's go for bi.

BOB.   No, we will not go for bi.

JOSH.   Well, then, I gotta tell you I am stumped. For now! But I am going to work on this, and I think in two months, tops, we'll have a word that we can work with. Of course, you may be *dead* by then —

BOB.   I love your Aunt Sally very much, Josh.

JOSH.   Hey, Bob, I'm sure you do.

BOB.   Don't you patronize me! Not on this subject!

JOSH.   How can I patronize you, you have nothing to *sell!*

BOB.   That's very good!

JOSH.   Thank you!

BOB.   No, that's *very* good, but what is *interesting* about it is how you go to word games when the subject turns to passion that is heterosexual —

JOSH.   You know, Bob, if I'm not mistaken I think you're on a *train of thought* —

BOB.   Well, tell me what you think that train of —

JOSH.   I think you're thinking Josh has not talked about a girlfriend, Josh in fact has *never* talked about a girlfriend —

BOB.   That's interesting, because I never said —

JOSH.   — but, see, I don't like guys, young guys, who hang out with their faggot uncles and talk about their girlfriends, I think it's *mean* —

BOB.   Josh, do you have a girlfriend?

JOSH.   What?

BOB.   Quick. In two seconds.

JOSH.   In two seconds the answer to that one is "yes."

BOB.   So you mean if I gave you *five* seconds —

JOSH.   In five seconds I would say I'm into tits and ass! What *is* —

BOB.   I am not talking about the mechanics of your sexuality!

JOSH.   Then rephrase the fucking question, will you, Bob?

BOB.   The question is, do you have any sense at all of what it means to have communion with a woman — and I mean sexual, spiritual and intellectual communion — no, let's scrap that, let's not get too ambitious here, Josh, have you ever had a *conversation* with a woman? A great critic, a great film critic, when he was writing for the *Village Voice,* said there is nothing more cinematic in the movies than a man and a woman talking to each other. That thought, like all great thoughts, has changed me, Josh, no, no, it has redeemed me. And, Josh, listen to this, now. Conversation does not *rule out* sex. Conversation can *blossom in*to sex. Conversation can even be sexual *in itself,* and I mean conversation about anything, about politics, or Hemingway, or the rain, or being exhausted. All this can be sexual, and I don't mean flirtation, I mean sex, so that the act, the sexual act, is not a break, a shock from all the talking, it's a *chord change.* All this can be yours, Josh, *if you learn to talk* —

JOSH.   Yeah, well, maybe you can talk about Hemingway or whatever with Aunt Sally, or those English teacher ladies that you slept around with back home, or with *whoever,* Bob, but I tell you, my girlfriend thinks that I'm a fucking *toy.*

BOB.   Well, Josh, I don't know how to say this, but you *are* a toy.

JOSH.   Look —

BOB.   In fact, it's possible you passed the moment years ago when you had any future as a heterosexual.

JOSH.   HEY!

BOB.   Oh, don't get so excited! Please! Don't get so predictable! What I'm saying is not as awful as you think, I'm only saying you have no future as a sexual being of any kind! Oh, you can *fuck,* Josh —

JOSH. Wait a minute! Wait! Are *you* deciding who's a sexual —

BOB. You mean because I had a few unfortunate encounters?

JOSH. A *few unfortunate* —

BOB. Josh, can I put your mind to rest about this? —

JOSH. Can you put my *mind* to rest? No, Bob, you can never put my mind to rest about this, no! —

BOB. Josh, they were nothing.

JOSH. *What?*

BOB. Nothing! They were —

JOSH. You're disgusting! You're pathetic! —

BOB. No, I'm not —

JOSH. I mean, you are this married faggot on the street and these guys brought you *comfort!*

BOB. What? Oh, please! *Please!* —

JOSH. Bob, they brought you comfort! Face it, Bob! They —

BOB. Josh, I am not Snow White and they were not the seven dwarfs!

JOSH. I'm saying these guys paid you some serious attention! —

BOB. It was five minutes! I don't believe this! Josh, this —

JOSH. *(Overlap.)* Five — five minutes is all you *set aside* for —

BOB. — this sentimentality is your most repellent quality, in a crowded field of nominees! —

JOSH. Yeah, yeah, well, like I say five minutes is the most you set aside for any comfort, Bob. OK, one time maybe Sally made it up to ten —

BOB. Sally has given me comfort all my life! —

JOSH. Oh, if she's given you all this comfort why is she *gone*, Bob?

BOB. She's gone because I'm difficult to live with! She's gone because I finally got her past the sentimentality of staying with me because I'm ill! She's gone because I would not let her be of help, which is like depriving Sally of her *protein!* Don't ask me these idiotic questions, Josh, they are a *waste* —

JOSH. OK, Bob, fine, I'm not going to ask you any questions. No more. And you know why I'm never going to ask you questions anymore? Because when I ask you questions, Bob, you answer me. And it is like *ridiculous.* Like "Josh, these guys" — I mean, all of a sudden it's guys, am I right? *All of a sudden,* or did I *drop a stitch?* —

BOB.   You did not drop a stitch, Josh, yes, it was sudden. And brief, sudden and —

JOSH.   OK, OK, I get it! But anyway, it's "Josh, these guys were nothing," except, Bob, they killed you. I mean, I'm sure you didn't *plan* for that, but, look, they killed you and you're dead, and what am I supposed to do now? Except, *fuck,* that's a *question,* and I *promised* —

BOB.   Do what you'd do without me, Josh. Go back home and get your Dad to get another Porsche for you and find the bridge you're waiting to drive off of and just do it. There. I've said it. But I will tell you this. Don't drive over the divider when you do it. Try to remember when you go to smash yourself that there are other people on the road. *(Pause.)* There. I've said it.

JOSH.   Yeah, that's cool.

BOB.   So let me read now.

JOSH.   Go ahead. *(Bob starts to, then:)*

BOB.   Look, I didn't mean I *want* you to drive off a bridge —

JOSH.   Bob, it's cool.

BOB.   Look, why don't you cook our dinner? You're an adequate cook, you really are.

JOSH.   I bought a fucking steak.

BOB.   Well, good, Josh. Cook it.

JOSH.   OK. *(Goes into kitchen, with steak; reappears.)* It's like thawing. OK?

BOB.   Fine.

JOSH.   See, I'd ask him for another Porsche —

BOB.   I didn't *mean* that —

JOSH.   — but the problem is he has no money, because he spends his money paying for you to live in *New York* —

BOB.   Oh, I see.

JOSH.   No, go ahead, Bob. Read.

BOB.   So it upsets you I live off your father.

JOSH.   Don't get so *excited,* Bob.

BOB. I've never been so calm. Josh, what do you live off?

JOSH. Well, not my Dad. OK, unless you count my *room*.

BOB. Yes, yes, but who? What?

JOSH. Look, unemployment! OK, I live off the taxpayer! Is that your p*oint*? Oh, this is brilliant, this is like the fucking *debates*. But, Bob, I don't hate the people I live off of.

BOB. I don't hate your Dad.

JOSH. Aw, man —

BOB. I love your Dad.

JOSH. Bob, you have got to stop this *mind-fucking* that you do —

BOB. Your Dad and I played together, Josh.

JOSH. Oh, well, the thought of that just makes me want to go on *drugs*.

BOB. We listened to the radio together.

JOSH. Bob, I don't care!

BOB. Well, I care! I CARE! This is my childhood we're talking about! I had one, too, you know! Fuck you, Josh, I care!

JOSH. OK! OK, what did you listen to? Keep in mind I don't believe a *word* of this.

BOB. *Gangbusters.*

JOSH. I'm not going to say a *thing*.

BOB. We listened to it Saturday nights at nine o'clock, and every time, at nine-fifteen, we ran down to the kitchen during the commercial and we ate a bowl of Grape Nuts, each, because we knew that at that moment that is what the commercial was telling us to do. And we ate in rhythm with each other and we finished just in time, so we could wash the bowls and get back up there just as the program was resuming — oh, shit! *(He is suddenly sobbing.)* This is ridiculous! I don't accept this!

JOSH. Hey —

BOB. Shut up, Josh! Just shut up!

JOSH. Are you *all right*?

BOB. Look, I resent this! I resent you!

JOSH. Well, look, that's OK, I resent you, too. Hey, Bob, it's OK, take a Kleenex — *(Which he produces from the bag.)* See I bought Kleenex. I knew that you were going to cry. I mean, you're *dying*, you know? And, see, I'll tell you something, Kleenex wasn't on your *list*. Think about it, Bob. And all I'm saying is, please don't take his money —

BOB.   But I want to take his money!

JOSH.   But he hates you!

BOB.   No, he doesn't hate me, he hates you! I hate to tell it to you, Josh, but deep down, under that *concerned exterior* —

JOSH.   He doesn't hate me, Bob, he has contempt for me. It's cool. Are you OK, Bob? He calls me like into his study, which he calls the family room, with pictures on the wall like of your Dad, the fucking *Titan*, you know? And pictures of you, Bob, you in *Hamlet* in college, and your reviews when you played Hamlet where it said you were *complex*, and you in eighth grade at some *typewriter* typing up some *novel*, then pictures of you and your like Mom and Dad sitting around the table after dinner while you *read* your novel, but my Dad's not in the pictures because he *took* the fucking pictures, and now he's sitting in the family room and *looking* at the pictures, and he talks to me, and, you know, smokes his *pipe*. He doesn't hate me, Bob. Where do you get off saying he hates me?

BOB.   All right, he doesn't hate you. He's just bewildered and saddened by the fact of your existence. No, no, that's harsh.

JOSH.   Yeah, see, that's *harsh*, Bob. I mean, see, you get carried away. It's more like — it's like Grandma, once, oh, just, well, after high school, I was at her house? Because with Mom and Dad, well, conversation had just broken *down*? And I was living at Grandma's and one night I was sleeping, except I wasn't? And she just stood there in the doorway and I heard her say — not angry, just, well, bewildered and sad, but *firm*, you know? She said, "Where have we failed?" That's what Dad feels. Where have we failed? It's not the fact of my *existence*. You're just so *heavy*, Bob. Come home with me.

BOB.   What?

JOSH.   Come home with me.

BOB.   Josh —

JOSH.   I don't like it here. Come on, Bob, please.

BOB.   So that's why you came here.

JOSH.   What?

BOB.   Did your father put you up to this? Because —

JOSH.   Hey, fuck off!

BOB.   It was a simple question.

JOSH.   This was my idea! I had an idea, is that so hard to *grasp?*

BOB.   Josh, if you think I'm going to move in with your father and your mother —

JOSH.   You'd have your own place, Bob!

BOB.   My own *place?*

JOSH.   Yes!

BOB.   A *condo?*

JOSH.   Sure a condo!

BOB.   Would it be in town?

JOSH.   Of course not! Nothing is in *town,* Bob!

BOB.   I refuse to live in a condo in the countryside! How can you —

JOSH.   Hey, Bob, you think I'd let you live with Mom and Dad? The way you talk to me? They wouldn't *get* it, Bob. No, you'd have your *own place,* and we could *hang,* and I would *shop* for you, and you could be boring and vicious like you *are!*

BOB.   Josh, listen to me! Listen! I thought you *understood* me! —

JOSH.   I am the *only* one who —

BOB.   I'd be in the same county with them! They would be kind to me, they'd try to comprehend me, they would actually *forgive* me for the one thing I am proud of in my life, which is its total, uncompromising, bracing failure! They would kill me within weeks, and I want more than weeks! What are you trying to *do* to me? —

JOSH.   But, Bob, Dad thinks you're a success. *(Pause.)*

BOB.   What?

JOSH.   I didn't want to be the one to break it to you.

BOB.   He thinks I'm a *success?*

JOSH.   He thinks you're brilliant. Face the music, Bob.

BOB.   The music? What music? What are you *saying?*

JOSH.   Bob, you were writing novels in the eighth grade.

BOB.   Well, doesn't that *tell* you anything? —

JOSH.   He thinks you're winning, Bob.

BOB.   He still thinks I'm winning? Jesus Christ, what does he *want?*

JOSH.   Oh, Bob, Uncle Bob, you are so full of shit.

BOB.   No, why. That's all I want to know. How could a smart man —

JOSH.   He thinks you're winning because he's running your Dad's company and his customers are buying from *Taiwan.* Bob, don't you read that *stuff* he sends you, those *reports?* So he's *laying off,* people who worked there for your *Dad,* and he wanted to be *like* your Dad, he wanted to be a fucking *savior* in the town —

BOB.   Our Dad was not a savior —

JOSH.   Will you let me finish?

BOB.   — He ran a company in good times and that is not in itself a religious act. Your father sentimentalizes everything, he always *has* —

JOSH.   Leave my father alone. Please? So he is up shit's creek, and Mom keeps putting on these *plays,* she keeps putting on *The Glass Menagerie,* and the only ones who come to see it are these *outpatients* from this psychiatric ward who fought in Vietnam, these fucking *bruisers,* Bob, who bawl their eyes out every time that guy knocks that girl's unicorn off the table. And there are fewer and fewer of those because they *overdose* and everybody else stays home and watches *cable.* And Mom says, "Where is community anymore?" and Dad is *hated,* but he thinks, "OK, I've got one thing, I have this brother who is *brilliant,* who's followed his own drummer or some fucking thing, and I am helping him. And one day he is going to *break through,* and he is going to be on *Larry King.*

BOB.   Josh, you said he hated me. You stood there and you said —

JOSH.   Sometimes he does! He's not *insane,* Bob! But, Bob, he takes you seriously and there is not a lot of that that's going *around!* And of course he hates you now and then, I mean, and not to criticize, you're *bleeding* him! —

BOB.   I bleed him so he'll stop believing in me, Josh. *(Pause.)*

35

JOSH. Oh —

BOB. I thought I succeeded, years ago. Josh, Josh. My writing was never any *good*.

JOSH. Wait — Bob, this is so sick. I mean, it's cool! —

BOB. Those novels in the eighth grade? Those early works? Josh, those were imitations. I wrote novels in the manner of the greats, and my family read them, and we sat around the table and *discussed* them. *Seriously.* Josh, my paternal grandmother said I had a mind as crystalline, as *focused,* as the mind of Dwight D. Eisenhower. And your poor father. He must have thought that he was going mad, because the only thing he heard was what a mind I had and there was no evidence of this of any kind. And the only way to keep his sanity was just to take those pictures, which were of the night, I think, they told me that the William Faulkner imitation was my best work yet. And then I was unstoppable, and the next year I wrote a novel in the manner of late Henry James. Do you know how *hard* that is? And they plowed through that and we discussed it, and your father never said a word, and never has, not all these years, but, Josh, I have gone *nowhere*. Does this mean nothing? My life has revealed that I was brilliant, yes, that I had promise, yes, but that I had no talent of my own of any kind. Am I to get no recognition for this? I came out of college to New York to *try my hand,* and, Josh, my failure was *complete*. And still, still they would not believe it. And when our father died you know who called me back to run the company? Me? Your father, who had wanted it himself since he was *small,* and I came, and within months I had brought it to its *knees*. And finally your father stepped in, sadly, Josh, *reluctantly,* and turned it around as much as it was possible to do, and, Josh, he *kept me on*. To work with him, to advise him, to lend my Eisenhower-like precision bomber of a mind to the D-Day he was launching against the ruinous decline that I had started, and which enriched I'm sure the disintegration of the whole economy, and I, of course, was a *fiasco.* I sat in board meetings, and pretended to take notes, and worked on something in the style of *Billy Budd,* and now and then asked questions that revealed I had not grasped one thing that had been said in half an hour, or indeed one thing that had happened in the world since 1950. And that was when I started sleeping with your English teachers, fine women, all of them, and I would show them what I'd written at the board meetings, and they'd tell me, "Bob, declare yourself! You have such passion, let the world know who you really are!" And your poor frantic mother put on *Harvey* for me, and, Josh, the rest is silence. Silence! And is it possible that you've come here to penetrate that silence? Is it possible you look to me for *anything*? Because if you do, I tell you, this is the first time I have actually *worried* about you.

JOSH.   So what you're saying is you committed fucking suicide because you didn't like the board meetings.

BOB.   What? Wait —

JOSH.   I'm not the suicide. You're the fucking suicide.

BOB.   Do you have the nerve to tell me? —

JOSH.   Yes.

BOB.   Josh, I am not telling you I am a suicide, I'm telling you I am a failure! A failure! —

JOSH.   And you are so fucking smug about it.

BOB.   Wait a minute! —

JOSH.   No! Bob! You have talked enough! I'm going to cook the steak, and you just sit here and you read your fucking *Hemingway* and *get off* on how it's all so clear how he was going to put a bullet through his head —

BOB.   Josh! —

JOSH.   The *stupid fuck!*

BOB.   Look, what do you want from me? *(Josh exits.)* You idiot! You want to use me as a *role model?*

JOSH.   *(Re-enters; very quiet.)* See, there you go. You know what you're doing? You're using words. You're using words, Bob.

BOB.   Forgive me, Josh, I —

JOSH.   And there you go again. Shut up. I say something, then you use some phrases, some fucking phrase, oh, you have got me so! pissed! off! I'm going to break something, I — no, I'm going to dress the steak, I'm going to slice the vegetables, I'm going to chop the fucking salad — *(He's gone to*

37

the kitchen. He returns and works on all this food while:) — but what I'm saying is you do that, you use some phrase that makes what I just said sound like I'm *young* or something, but I'm *not young,* I'm older than you are, you don't know what's going on, you sit here, you don't even *go out* except to get infected, and why did you do that, Bob? No, don't tell me. I'll bet you thought it was some great *rebellion,* some big *idea* or something, some existential fucking thing, I'll bet you sat here wearing a *beret* and thought, "I know, I'll go out there and fuck some *guys* and maybe I'll get AIDS and maybe *not,* I mean it's all so meaningless, so *hey!*" I'll bet you were *reading* when you thought that. Where's the book? Which one? I want to see the book! *(He is ripping the books off the shelf.)* But, no. Come on, Josh. Don't get so excited. It's over now, it's *over.* And I'll bet you thought it was soooo radical, I'll bet you thought we'd say, "Hey, thanks, Bob! Thanks for showing us how meaningless the whole thing is," well, Bob, I got to tell you, Bob, we *knew* that. You stupid *shit,* Bob. And this disease you got yourself, I've worked in *wards,* and, Bob, you are an idiot, you do not know what's down the road for you. It's not going to be existential, Bob, it's going to *suck.* But that is what I like about you, Bob, that it's a *stance.* I mean, everybody else gets AIDS because they're *bored,* but you get AIDS because you think it *philosophically fits in.* It's not like where I live, they just don't think that way out there, and I got to tell you, I'm going crazy there, and, Bob, you're right, I want to wreck another Porsche, Bob, I can *feel* it, it feels like wanting to get *laid,* I *want* it, so you come home and talk to Dad, *quick,* and sit there in that house where you grew up, *sit in the family room,* and think about the way you blew it. Then you won't die saying, "Oh, it's all so meaningless," with some smug smile across your face, you'll die *pissed off,* and then I'll think this guy was not a suicide, this guy was brilliant, but it was all too much for him so he became an outlaw and a flop. I think that would be *beautiful.* That would be something I could *shoot* for. I want you in a *rage!* And I don't mean a *snit* like you're in now, I mean a *rage,* and that will calm me down, it will, you gotta trust me, that will make me happy. My life is in your fucking *hands,* Bob, isn't that a thrill? Tell me that doesn't turn you on. *(Pause.)*

BOB.   Well.

JOSH.   Yeah. So, anyway, come home with me.

BOB.   You knew that Sally had moved out before you came here. Didn't you.

JOSH.   What?

BOB.   You knew I was alone before you came to see me.

JOSH.   What are you saying?

BOB.   I'm saying you pretended that you didn't know, and that you knew, and that you came, you hitched here in your — did you wear that T-shirt?

JOSH.   Hey, it's August.

BOB.   I see. It's August.

JOSH.   You know, I'm gonna say it. I'm gonna lay it out. I think you're hitting on me, Uncle Bob.

BOB.   I've lusted for you since you were eight.

JOSH.   Since I was eight.

BOB.   But then you knew that.

JOSH.   Since I was eight?

BOB.   All right, you didn't know it then, not consciously.

JOSH.   I mean, when I was nine I knew it.

BOB.   Nine?

JOSH.   Yeah, what the fuck.

BOB.   You knew when you were *nine* that —

JOSH.   I was swift, Bob.

BOB.   That's disgusting.

JOSH.   Let's cut to the chase here, Uncle Bob. OK? See, you think I go that way. You think because I knew Aunt Sally had moved out, and I made out I didn't know, and because I wear a *T*-shirt, you think I go that way. Well, Bob, your thinking is fucked. See, Bob, I look up to you. I always have. And when you look up to some guy and you know you turn him on, it's like a *buzz,* it's *nice,* that's all, particularly if you think he's like in general straight. So, Bob, I do not go that way but even if I did, *you have AIDS.* Do you *forget?* And I know, they've got safe sex, but, Uncle Bob, it doesn't sound like you're an *expert* on that, and let me give it to you straight, I'm not like *in* to having AIDS —

BOB. Excuses, excuses.

JOSH. Right, Bob.

BOB. Why did you come here? Tell me. And this is not a trick question —

JOSH. I came to visit you. I came to help you out. I had this feeling you were all alone. It was a Christian gesture, Bob. See, you don't know this, nobody knows this, I applied to be assistant chaplain on this battleship and, OK, they turned me down, on grounds of, like, well, mental health, but I thought, shit! I have this fucking goodness in my heart, it's going to bum me out, what do I *do* with it? And then I thought, I know, I have this uncle who can't cross the *street,* and like I say he's all alone. I mean, is that OK? Is that *cool?* Are you *all right* about this?

BOB. I am furious.

JOSH. Yeah.

BOB. It's nothing personal, it's not you. Just get out of here.

JOSH. OK, I'll go out for a while. Bob?

BOB. What?

JOSH. Get a life. And I'm not joking, that's not some stupid *joke.* I know what I'm talking about. Get a life, Bob. I mean — *(He stops. Bob says nothing. So Josh goes. Bob sits there. Lights.)*

SCENE 3

Morning. Bob is going through things. Josh enters.

JOSH. Hey, Bob!

BOB. Good morning, Josh.

JOSH. Good morning. *(Bob works.)* What are you doing?

BOB. I'm going through my *glossies.*

JOSH. What? Pictures?

BOB. Yes.

JOSH. *(Looks.)* Those are pictures of you, Bob.

BOB. That's right.

JOSH. Yeah. *(Pause.)* Why are you doing this?

BOB. Because, you know, Josh? I don't get out much.

JOSH. Well, I've been *telling* you this —

BOB. Well, you are not the only one.

JOSH. I didn't say I was the only one —

BOB. Aunt Sally, for example, has —

JOSH. Well, sure she has —

BOB. Just last night, as a matter of fact, she —

JOSH. Last night? —

BOB. She came over last night, and she —

JOSH. She came over? —

BOB. Yes, and —

JOSH. Just like that?

BOB. Well, no. What? —

JOSH. No, she — anyway —

BOB. Anyway, she —

JOSH. You called her, didn't you.

BOB. Well — yes —

JOSH. Like how soon after I walked out the door?

BOB. Oh — what? — five minutes —

JOSH. OK.

BOB. My point is —

JOSH. Can I have some coffee?

BOB. You don't have to ask me if you — *(As Josh pours.)* I don't think you need that coffee.

JOSH. Look, just, I will be the judge of that.

BOB. Where have you been all night?

JOSH. See, I've been drinking coffee, fine, OK? But I've been like drinking it in Styrofoam —

BOB. Where have you —

JOSH. I've been where they have Styrofoam! What does it matter where I've been exactly, as long as you know they have Styrofoam? I mean, you know it's not the fucking Oak Room, OK? It's not Mostly Fucking Mozart! OK? —

BOB. Put down that cup —

JOSH. No, I will not put down this cup. This cup is pretty. This cup is — grey! —

BOB.   You have been sitting up all night in —

JOSH.   Burger King! And it's the first time in this fucking city that I've been like *relaxed,* that I thought, OK, Josh, you're *home!* —

BOB.   You were not relaxed, don't lie to me.

JOSH.   I was relaxed!

BOB.   You were terrified that if you came home your Uncle Bob would take you *by force* —

JOSH.   You think — wait — you really think I'm sitting up in Burger King from *fear?*

BOB.   Yes!

JOSH.   Boredom! Boredom, Bob! I thought I'll come here, and you'll be in your bedroom and you'll *hear* me come in and you'll pretend to be asleep and then I'll *turn in* and I'll pretend to be asleep and we'll like *breathe* all night —

BOB.   Well, you were wrong.

JOSH.   Well, yes, I guess I *was.* I mean, you're like *adaptable* —

BOB.   That's right, Josh.

JOSH.   So what you're trying to tell me is that you and Aunt Sally *got it on* —

BOB.   Look, just suffice it to say —

JOSH.   Oh, that is gross. That is *so sad.*

BOB.   No, it is not —

JOSH.   Bob, is she safe?

BOB.   What?

JOSH.   Aunt Sally. Is she going to be OK?

BOB.   Of course she is. What are you —

JOSH.   Do you *know* that, Bob?

BOB.   Well, I'll tell you this, I'm not going to draw you a picture.

JOSH.   Well, good. Good. Because if you like infected her —

BOB.   I don't know why I'm discussing this with you —

JOSH.   Because you couldn't wait to bring it up, that's why! Because you must have gone at it all night hoping you'd hear my key so you could come out in your *robe* and say, "Is that you, Josh? Lock up before you go to bed. I've got Sally in there now, we'll talk in the morning," then I'm supposed to lie awake thinking, "Boy, Josh, you had it all wrong! This guy is not a *dweeb!* This guy has *moved on! —*

BOB.   I would think you'd be relieved, Josh!

JOSH.   Don't get smart with me! Don't get smug! You want to know the truth? I think it's great you called Aunt Sally. I hope you sent her my *regards —*

BOB.   I did.

JOSH.   Well, *good.*

BOB.   She sent her very best to you.

JOSH.   Well, good.

BOB.   She said since you're clearly looking for a homeless shelter, you should come and see her, she could set you up somewhere —

JOSH.   So anyway you did it with Aunt Sally all night, then you went out and got your *glossies —*

BOB.   I had my glossies, Josh. You don't get glossies in the middle of the night.

JOSH.   Look, I didn't mean! —

BOB.   You don't know what you mean! I'll tell you what you mean. That's all I do, is tell you what you mean, and that is not how I had thought to pass my last days on this earth —

JOSH.   What did I mean, then, Bob, I mean, I'm really *anxious —*

BOB.   You meant you're jealous of Aunt Sally, you —

JOSH.   Aw, wait a minute! —

BOB.   I will not wait a minute, there is *no time —*

JOSH.   Bob! —

BOB.   You stand there and demean last night, you say I did it with Sally and then went and got my glossies as if that were all there was to it, well, Sally came here and we fought! We *fought,* Josh! We didn't snipe at each other, which is all that ever happens when I see you. We fought and Sally saw to it that I got myself up, that I *try* something —

JOSH.   I told you get a life!

BOB.   Well, I prefer the same information coming from Aunt Sally. All right? Get that paper over there.

JOSH.   You get that paper yourself!

BOB.   Josh, if you want to know what happened between

43

Sally and me —

JOSH.   Bob, do you think I care? —

BOB.   — the first place to look is in that paper. Besides, I need —

JOSH.   *(Overlap.)* What? Where?

BOB.   I need some information —

JOSH.   This paper is *Backstage*. It's called *Backstage*.

BOB.   That's right. Now, just —

JOSH.   Sally brought this?

BOB.   Yes, she did. And what I need —

JOSH.   You called Aunt Sally to come over and have sex and she brought *Backstage?*

BOB.   No, she went back for it. Now, I want you to look up —

JOSH.   Wait, she went back? It was raining! —

BOB.   I told you that we fought! She was exercised! Look, I don't want to talk to you about this, you wouldn't understand it anyway, all I want from you is an address —

JOSH.   Bob, I know what happened! You think I don't know what happened? I can picture it! I know just what you fought about, it's like renting a movie you've already seen because the one you want to see is *out* —

BOB.   You know nothing! I'm going to change! — *(Starts to get up.)*

JOSH.   I know everything! I know it all! Sally dropped everything, she took the pasta she was cooking out of the oven, Bob, and brought it over to you, in the rain, but when she got here she wasn't like, "Bob, oh, Bob, are you all right, Bob?" She was *steamed* and she said, "Bob, what is it *now?*" and you said, "I am going to sit here, Sally, and I'm going to die, and I just wanted you to know that, Sally, and the reason is" — except you didn't say this part — "the reason is my nephew won't *put out*" and Sally said — *(As Bob leaves the room to change clothes.)* — no, wait, Bob! Sally said, "Well, you know that you don't have to sit there! You know there are things that you can do!" and you said this back and forth for like two hours, louder and louder, and you probably even *threw things,* and I'm supposed to be jealous of this? I'm supposed to get all weak thinking how *hot* this is? And, frankly, Bob, I *am,* that is how fucking bleak my life is, and finally you said, "What? What can I do? Name one thing I can do, you bitch!" And she got excited like we all do when you actually *ask* for something, and she said, "I'll show you! I'll go back in the rain and get *Backstage!"* — *(Of which he is now turning the pages.)* — it has these things in it about these *plays,* and these like *tryouts,* and how the fuck did Sally get *Backstage?* Oh, wait, I know, I'll bet they do plays in her *church,* I'll bet it's in the *basement,* I'll bet when they're not putting up the homeless they do Agatha Christie, I'll bet they do the fucking *Mousetrap* right there in Sally's church, I'll bet that's what she circled here, except, no, she circled — oh, no, Bob —

BOB. *(Enters, dressed for audition.)* What I want you to do is tell me the address of the audition —

JOSH. Bob, this is *Hamlet.*

BOB. I know it's *Hamlet,* and I'm not discussing —

JOSH. Bob, Bob, Hamlet is in *college! —*

BOB. Hamlet is thirty years old! The text explicitly states that he is thirty years old. Will you just give me the address? —

JOSH. OK! OK! Thirty years old, but, *Bob! —*

BOB. Sally remembers me in college in that play, and she was *moved —*

JOSH. OK. So Sally came back and she threw down *Backstage* and she circled *Hamlet* and you fucked like *rabbits —*

BOB. Josh, your grasp of the essential nature of last night is brilliant. Brilliant. You've even captured some of the tonalities. I want the address —

JOSH. Bob, please, please don't go out on this tryout, please! —

BOB. Oh, you don't understand. Hamlet is middle-aged, by the standards of his time he's middle-aged, a time of life that you, probably, will never know, Josh. He's in trouble, and do you know what he says about it? "Frailty, thy name is woman." Well, I have never called Aunt Sally frail, no one could ever call Aunt Sally emotionally frail, but I have called her corrupt. Of course I meant it as a compliment, but "corrupt?" Can you believe that? Sally, who is so much more remarkable, more *pure* than that idiotic woman in the play, and I have called her corrupt! I can play this part. I can play it now. Besides, they're doing it on Staten Island. I'm going to do it, Josh. When I did it in college everybody said that I was brilliant, but *even so* I think there's hope for it. I played it in the manner of Olivier, or was it Maurice Evans, *I* don't know, but I do know I didn't know a *thing*. But now I do. I know *something*. I know that I have AIDS, for instance. That is *information*. That is *knowledge*. I can *work* with that. That is not a novel in the manner of — who was it I was imitating *just last week?* — Marquez! That is my *own*. I'm dying, I love my wife, I've called her even worse than frail, and I can be a stunning Hamlet. Besides, as I say, it's Staten Island. Give me the address.

JOSH.   Well, here. Here it is, you look —

BOB.   Will you read it to me, please? —

JOSH.   Hey, I can't hold it still —

BOB.   It's all that coffee! —

JOSH.   I know it's all that coffee! —

BOB.   Look, will you control yourself and read it? Put it down on the table —

JOSH.   Hey! What is this?

BOB.   I thought you came to help me!

JOSH.   Bob, look, there is all this *information!* —

BOB.   Can't you just find the simple fucking address? Can't you just write it DOWN? In BIG LETTERS? Is that asking TOO MUCH?

JOSH.   Oh, shit —

BOB.   Or has that coffee so released the incoherence that is the essence of your soul —

JOSH.   Are you going blind?

BOB.   Of course I'm going blind! Don't you know *anything?* I thought you worked in *wards*, what did you do there, *read magazines?* —

JOSH.   Oh — FUCK! *(He smashes the coffee cup. Pause.)* OK, OK. Address. Here it is.

BOB.   Thank you.

JOSH.   Well, now, don't get up. I mean, you're going to step

46

in all these *shards*. If you'll just *sit* a minute I'll like clean this up —

BOB. You don't have to clean it up.

JOSH. Oh, yes, I *do,* Bob. Yes, I *do.* Just, where's the dust-pan?

BOB. I think it's terrible you don't know where the dust-pan is. I think it's terrifying —

JOSH. So do I, Bob.

BOB. It's in the closet. Don't you have any capacity to think things through? I mean, I *grieve* for you, I grieve for the life you're going to lead.

JOSH. Hey. Bob. I'm way ahead of you. *(Pause.)* I'll get the dustpan. *(Goes; returns with dustpan.)* There. Now. I'm sweeping up the pieces.

BOB. Without a *broom?*

JOSH. I couldn't find the broom.

BOB. The broom is there. It's right there. And I wonder what has happened to our family. Now, get the broom. You're going to cut your fingers, don't you *know* that?

JOSH. Shit!

BOB. What?

JOSH. I cut my finger.

BOB. Oh, my God. My God. All right, all right. Don't move. Just sit there. I'm going to the medicine cabinet. I'm going to get some hydrogen peroxide.

JOSH. Bob, you can't *see* —

BOB. *(Goes.)* I said that I was *going* blind. I didn't say I *was* blind. I'm going to get some Band-Aids —

JOSH. That's OK, Bob, really —

BOB. *(Reappears.)* No, it's not OK. It's not OK for you to sit and *bleed* —

JOSH. Bob, I can do it.

BOB. I know you *can,* but I don't think you *will* —

JOSH. I can do it. Look. I'm sucking on it. Please

BOB. Give me your hand.

JOSH. No —

BOB. *(Grabs his hand.)* Oh, for Christ's sake, give me —

JOSH. Bob, that's an open cut, just get away! —

BOB.   Stop pulling! —

JOSH.   Let go!

BOB.   *(Not letting go.)* Josh. Look. Look at my hand. See? There's not a scratch —

JOSH.   Yeah, but there's —

BOB.   What?

JOSH.   Fluids!

BOB.   There are no fluids!

JOSH.   Oh, fuck you, you're going to kill me!

BOB.   Open that hand, Josh! *(Forces it.)*

JOSH.   Oh, shit!

BOB.   There now, I've got the peroxide on the cotton, I'm putting the cotton on your hand —

JOSH.   Help!

BOB.   And now I'm putting on the ointment —

JOSH.   *(Genuine terror.)* HELP! HELP!

BOB.   I'm doing this, Josh! And here's the Band-Aid — *(Suddenly Josh leaps up and grabs Bob, pushes him against the wall, and begins to beat him.)*

JOSH.   You — faggot! — you're not going to kill me, you — you! —

BOB.   *(Overlap.)* Josh? — what? — stop that! — JOSH! — *(Starts out of the room, into the hall.)*

JOSH.   *(Stops him.)* How did you get it up with Sally? Did you think of me? —

BOB.   No, I did not! — *(Pulls away; goes off.)*

JOSH.   *(Follows him. We hear things crashing, as the beating continues.)* You thought of me! You make me sick! — You fucked her and you made her sick! —

BOB.   *(Tries to get out the front door.)* STOP!

JOSH.   *(Prevents him from getting out the door.)* You infected her! And you did it so you could think that it was me!

BOB.   *(Runs to window, yells out of it.)* HELP!

JOSH.   *(Pulls him from window, hugs him from behind.)* Oh, shit! You were the only one I ever loved! You didn't *care.* You were the only one that I could *talk* to. It was like nothing *mattered* to you and it saved my ass — you sick *killer!* — faggot! — *(He has pushed Bob down; he stands over him.)* — oh, shit. Oh, shit.

(Josh pulls Bob up; for a moment they don't move.)

BOB. *(After a long pause.)* I'm going now. Are you all right?

JOSH. Fuck you.

BOB. Yes.

JOSH. Good luck.

BOB. Thank you. *(Pause.)* Are you all right? *(Josh doesn't answer. Bob leaves. Josh roams the room, picks up after the fight and at one point can't get back up off the floor. But then he does, and he goes to the window and looks out, thinking, for a long moment, before the lights go out.)*

SCENE 4

Later. Late afternoon. Josh sits there. Bob enters.

BOB. Hello, Josh.

JOSH. Hey, Bob.

BOB. Hey.

JOSH. You were there a long time.

BOB. Well, there was a *line.*

JOSH. So lots of people want to act in *Hamlet* out on Staten Island.

BOB. Yes.

JOSH. Well, why not? You know?

BOB. That's what I say. I admired them.

JOSH. Yeah, I admire that.

BOB. I mean, most of them were out of work. I don't mean out of work actors, I mean school teachers. People who no doubt had been teaching in the *arts.* Or sanitation workers.

JOSH. Cool.

BOB. Yes.

JOSH. So. You going to *get* it?

BOB. No.

JOSH. *(Gentle.)* Well, like, see, there you *go,* Bob.

BOB. That's right.

JOSH. This *thing* you do. This thing about you don't have

49

any talent.

BOB. I didn't show them my talent.

JOSH. What? —

BOB. It didn't get that far.

JOSH. Oh, what did you do?

BOB. I showed them my *mind*.

JOSH. Oh, shit.

BOB. That's right.

JOSH. What did you *say*? I'll bet you *said* something.

BOB. I said something because I *had* to. They were not going to let me do anything for them. They got to me at five o'clock, and they said, "Oh, we're sorry, but this isn't *right*" —

JOSH. Well, did you tell them how Hamlet's like this old man? —

BOB. Yes! I said, "I suppose you think that he's this young prince, right?" And they said, "Well, yes, we —" and I said, "Stop the production! Stop right now!" And they said, "What?" And I said, "Don't you see what you are doing? You are idealizing him! And don't you see what he is, he hates women, he is afraid of women, and for centuries he's been regarded as the finest, the fairest, the most brilliant man in Western culture, the spokesman for our whole civilization, and he's sick! But no one will admit it, and unless we do we're *doomed!* Oh, God," I cried, "Please! Please believe me! I can show you, I can do it for you, please don't cast some fucking sensitive young man, don't keep glorifying this *rot!*" —

JOSH. What did they like do at this point?

BOB. They thanked me for my insights. They thought my mind was brilliant. And I said, "My mind? My *mind?* This is not my *mind!*" And I left.

JOSH. Bob, you should go into acting. I don't mean like Staten Island, you should —

BOB. Josh, I have no *skills!*

JOSH. How do you *know* that?

BOB. Because I've never developed any skills!

JOSH. That doesn't matter, Bob! I mean like does that *matter*? None of those people, none of them have any *skills*, Bob. I mean, do you believe anything you see them do, ever?

50

That's what you mean by skills, isn't it, that you believe them, but, come on, what's there to *believe?* The only thing that they can do that means anything is when they make you laugh, and, OK, Bob, you can't do that, I mean that play about the rabbit was *depressing* when you did it, I mean the way you drank and cried about that rabbit, Bob, it was a *bad night.* But, Bob, OK, stay out of comedies, but you can do that other shit, and, sure, nobody would believe you, but *so what?* But anyway, we gotta, not to beat around the bush, we gotta put this on the table. Bob, I beat the *shit* out of you this morning, and we haven't even *mentioned* it.

BOB.   Oh, what's the point of *mentioning* it? —

JOSH.   Well, look, I can't tell you right offhand but there's got to be some *point.* But maybe there isn't. *I* don't know. I mean, you're not like *injured,* are you?

BOB.   Well, I'm bruised, I think —

JOSH.   I don't mean *bruised,* I mean fucking *injured.* Get serious, Bob.

BOB.   Well, I went all the way to Staten Island.

JOSH.   Well, OK, then. But, still, it wasn't right, you know. I gotta say it. So I'd like to — you know — like make it up to you.

BOB.   Oh, please. No, please. Just — don't do it anymore, that's all. I don't know what you *say* on these occasions —

JOSH.   I mean, I'd like to — you know — make love to you. *(Pause.)*

BOB.   You see, now you've offended me.

JOSH.   Oh, fuck. Come on. Don't get *uptight.*

BOB.   Look. In the first place —

JOSH.   *In the first place?* What? Is there like going to be a *list?* I mean, you are pissing me off! —

BOB.   No, you are pissing *me* off —

JOSH.   OK, OK, but, look, I ought to warn you, I'm not planning to back off on this —

BOB.   Well, Josh, I think I ought to point out —

JOSH.   *Point out?* Point out *what?*

BOB.   That you need my consent for this to happen —

JOSH.   Well, I *know* that. You think I don't *know* that? But

I thought that wouldn't be a problem. I mean, you said you lusted after me since I was eight years old —

BOB.   But you're not — this is ridiculous! — you said you weren't —

JOSH.   What? Gay? Well, that's right, I'm not gay! I mean, it makes me sick, it makes me *retch* —

BOB.   Well, then —

JOSH.   But that will add to it!

BOB.   Add *what*?

JOSH.   Well, it will make it more — more like a *gift* or something! —

BOB.   This is sick! I mean, I knew that you were very troubled, I've always thought you needed —

JOSH.   Bob, I've had therapy. Come *on*. I've had therapy up the ass, Bob, if you'll pardon the expression —

BOB.   Oh, now, you're getting insolent! You're getting —

JOSH.   Bob, I don't think you're being like very *gracious* about this.

BOB.   All right, all right. You're right. Let's — this is very kind, I'm just taken aback, and — and, Josh, you *know*, elements of this have been my fantasy for many years. *Elements* of it. But, Josh, I must be fair, I must be honest, I — and this is my problem, I guess — with men — not with Aunt Sally, not with those women in the Art Guild back home, but particularly with Aunt Sally, because my feelings for Aunt Sally have an element of personal concern that — well, you know, they may be the one achievement that I —

JOSH.   Could you like get to the point, Bob?

BOB.   Yes, I can. My point is that with men I don't like safe sex. Which means that since I was infected I've abstained, Josh. Even if I'd wanted to, you see, it's not just that, as you put it — *unforgettably*, Josh — it's not just that I'm not an expert on it. *I don't like it.* And I don't mean *metaphorically*, I don't even mean emotionally —

JOSH.   No, I know what you mean, Bob —

BOB.   I mean physically. I like unsafe sex. And not because it's unsafe, although, come to think of it, that may be part of —

JOSH.   I didn't say it had to be safe sex. *(Pause.)*

BOB.   What?

JOSH.   I mean, I *figured,* you know, I *figured* you were into like the bad way, I mean *really,* because otherwise why would you have like gotten yourself into this stupid fucking situation.

BOB.   Wait a minute. What are you saying to me?

JOSH.   What do you mean, what am I saying to you? Do you want a fucking *diagram?* —

BOB.   Get out of here!

JOSH.   What? Hey! Chill!

BOB.   I don't believe this!

JOSH.   Look! You *said* to me, you said, don't drive over the dividing line! I mean, you *said* that! And like I *thought* about it. But, look, if you're going to kill yourself, and, let's face it, Bob, *I might,* I mean I won't like take a gun or anything but we all know I'll probably do the deed one way or other sometime before I'm *whatever* and I mean, what *difference* does it make, I mean, I don't want to be like *flip* or anything, I don't want a fucking *lecture* from you, Bob, but, OK, it means I'll miss a few more *episodes* of something, I don't know, I haven't really given it a lot of thought, but *anyway,* sure, don't drive over the dividing line, like I *agree* with you, I mean that's *murder* or some fucking thing, but, Bob, it's *boring* just to drive into a tree! I mean, I have been thinking all about this, see, you got me thinking, Bob, but then you always did, that's why I wanted you to come back home, I mean, I *hate* New York.

BOB.   Josh, you know what they call what you're —

JOSH.   Oh, who cares what they *call* it?

BOB.   Altruistic suicide.

JOSH.   OK, then, altruistic suicide, whatever *turns you on,* Bob.

BOB.   Wait! But, Josh. Listen to me. Altruistic suicide loses, well, its point when the person you're being altruistic to becomes the *weapon.* Don't you see? —

JOSH.   But you're lonely, man. You're going to die lonely. And you know? So am I. I mean, what are we *talking* about? I'm getting like *impatient* —

BOB.   Josh, I can't do this.

JOSH.   Yes, you can. You know you can. It's just you won't, and that's your whole life, Bob, I hate to have to say it, but that is your life, I mean about everything, it's just — you won't.

BOB.   Well, all right, then. Whatever.

JOSH.   So this is like — "no"?

BOB.   That's right.

JOSH.   I don't *believe* this!

BOB.   Neither do I, Josh. *(Pause.)*

JOSH.   No, I'm lying. I do believe it. In fact, look, I'm a little bit ahead of you.

BOB.   Josh, you're way ahead of me.

JOSH.   No, no, I mean I like took steps to get around this, because I thought, "Look, this is going to freak him out," so I — now don't get mad, OK? don't get like you *get* —

BOB.   What did you do?

JOSH.   Well, Bob. I went out and I got laid today. I mean, I like anticipated your objections so I —

BOB.   So you what?

JOSH.   So I —

BOB.   Josh. Are you telling me that you deliberately —

JOSH.   Yes, I'm telling you that I deliberately.

BOB.   Are you saying that you went cruising, Josh?

JOSH.   Cruising? *Cruising?* What are you *saying?* Bob, this is not the fucking nineteenth century! This is not like 1952! This is not some Al Pacino movie you can hardly *rent*, no, Bob, I did not *cruise*, what do you think I *am*, Bob? I went up to some guy who was like *coughing*, and I said, right out, Bob, I said, "Hey, you look like *shit*. Look, I'm sick, too, this sucks, doesn't it, so let's *get it on*" —

BOB.   What did he say?

JOSH.   Oh, he cried. You know. I mean, I don't think he was *expecting* this. So he like took my hand and took me up to this like room he lived in —

BOB.   I don't believe this. I don't believe a word of this.

JOSH.   Well, that's your *problem* then. If you can't like accept a simple gift what good are you? I mean, I know you're

54

no good, you keep *telling* me, but, really, Bob, what *good* are you?

BOB.   I'll tell you what good I am. I'm good enough not to give into this. This is a lie, Josh. And I always wondered what good I was, and now I know, I'm good enough not to believe this lie and do what you are asking me to do, even though I want to. And thank you, Josh. You've done a Christian act. Just by trying to get me to believe this lie you've done a Christian act. You don't have to take it any further. And that's a good thing, because this way you'll live, and you'll know how generous you are, and I don't think you've ever known how generous you are, I think that's why you've been so lost, so —

JOSH.   You want his number? I took his number.

BOB.   If he told me the whole thing, in detail, I would not believe him. I'd believe you told him what to say, and that he was so bewildered by that conversation —

JOSH.   Then I'll bring him here. We'll show you what we did. Oh, this is getting *gross*. And if you still don't believe me I will keep on doing it, every day, until I *pass muster*. You're insulting me. I mean, you've never been *nice* to me, which has been cool, but now you are insulting me. *Deeply,* Bob. And what are you getting for it? Loneliness. Which is all you've ever gotten for it. I mean, don't you learn anything? Ever? I mean, you might as well not even kill yourself if you're not going to take the trouble to learn something from it. *(Pause.)* Bob? *(Pause.)* Bob? *(Pause.)* Oh, shit, now I've done it. Now I've really done it. Now you're not going to talk to me.

BOB.   You should go home. Right now. Go home, let them take care of you. Right now, and take the bus, no, fly, fly, I'll pay for it, I've got some cash in there, it's hidden in the bedroom for whatever might come up for me, but fuck it, *fuck* it, bring it to me, it's under some shirts in the —

JOSH.   Bob, how can I go home? I am *infected*. All for you, and you don't even want it. Shit, it's the one good idea I ever had. *(Pause.)*

BOB.   Come here, Josh.

JOSH.   OK, I will. Just give me a minute, OK?

BOB.   Are you scared?

JOSH.   No, I'm not scared. Will you stop? No, I just want to take this in, that's all.

BOB.   All right.

JOSH.   All right, Bob. But I'll be there, I promise. Chill. *(Neither moves. Lights.)*

END OF PLAY

PROPERTY LIST

Lined pad
Pencils
Markers
Tape recorder (BOB)
Knapsack (JOSH)
Breakaway plate
Blanket (JOSH)
Wastebasket
D'Agostino grocery store bag (JOSH) with:
    various groceries
    receipt
Book: *The Sun Also Rises*
Kleenex tissues
Bowl with head of lettuce (JOSH)
Books
Box with 8 x 10 photographs of Uncle Bob
Styrofoam cup (JOSH)
Grey coffee cup (JOSH)
Backstage newspaper (JOSH)
Dustpan (JOSH)
Cotton (BOB)
Hydrogen peroxide (BOB)
Bandage (BOB)
Stage blood (BOB)

COSTUME PLOT

SCENES ONE AND TWO

BOB
Comfortable, long-sleeved, wine-colored shirt
Grey slacks
Khaki deck shoes
Khaki worn safari jacket

JOSH
Worn pants
Lace-up boots
Sleeveless denim jacket
Light-colored T-shirt (#1)
Traditional style (long sleeve and pants), worn as pajamas
L.A. Raiders cap
T-shirt #2
T-shirt #3
T-shirt #4 (form fitting or with some slightly vulgar imprint)

SCENES THREE AND FOUR

BOB
Navy bathrobe
T-shirt
Burgundy long-sleeved shirt
Burgundy cotton sweater-vest
Grey slacks
Khaki deck shoes

JOSH
Same as Scene One

NEW
PLAYS

**THE AFRICAN COMPANY PRESENTS
RICHARD III**
by Carlyle Brown

**EDWARD ALBEE'S
FRAGMENTS and THE MARRIAGE PLAY**

IMAGINARY LIFE
by Peter Parnell

MIXED EMOTIONS
by Richard Baer

THE SWAN
by Elizabeth Egloff

*Write for information as to
availability*
DRAMATISTS PLAY SERVICE, Inc.
440 Park Avenue South   New York, N.Y. 10016

NEW
PLAYS

THE LIGHTS
by Howard Korder

THE TRIUMPH OF LOVE
by James Magruder

LATER LIFE
by A.R. Gurney

THE LOMAN FAMILY PICNIC
by Donald Margulies

A PERFECT GANESH
by Terrence McNally

SPAIN
by Romulus Linney

Write for information as to availability
DRAMATISTS PLAY SERVICE, Inc.
440 Park Avenue South   New York, N.Y. 10016

NEW
PLAYS

LONELY PLANET
by Steven Dietz

THE AMERICA PLAY
by Suzan-Lori Parks

THE FOURTH WALL
by A.R. Gurney

JULIE JOHNSON
by Wendy Hammond

FOUR DOGS AND A BONE
by John Patrick Shanley

**DESDEMONA, A PLAY ABOUT A
HANDKERCHIEF**
by Paula Vogel

*Write for information as to
availability*
DRAMATISTS PLAY SERVICE, Inc.
440 Park Avenue South   New York, N.Y. 10016

NEW
PLAYS

THREE TALL WOMEN
by Edward Albee

BROKEN GLASS
by Arthur Miller

SUBURBIA
by Eric Bogosian

ALL IN THE TIMING
by David Ives

HELLO AGAIN
by Michael John LaChiusa

PTERODACTYLS
by Nicky Silver

*Write for information as to
availability*
DRAMATISTS PLAY SERVICE, Inc.
440 Park Avenue South   New York, N.Y. 10016

UNCLE BOB

by Austin Pendleton

2M

The uproariously articulate Uncle Bob lives alone in his small Greenwich Village apartment. Although he and his wife are totally devoted to one another, she's left him as she just can't put up with him anymore, yet he still speaks, at length, to her even though she's gone. This is fine with him — he's happy in his hermitage, until one evening, Josh, his nephew, turns up uninvited. Josh is a very unstable young man, possibly suicidal, probably dangerous and definitely unwelcome. It seems that all Josh wants to do is torture his reclusive uncle but he soon reveals the rather dubious real reason he's run away from home: he has come in order to convince Bob to return with him to his family so they can care for him. Bob has AIDS. Although Josh insists this is the true reason for his visit, both men know there are other reasons. They begin a bitter macabre dance as the true nature of their relationship slowly reveals itself. Even though they seem to detest each other, their need for acceptance and love soon overpowers them as they explore their self hatred and their hatred of others, accept their uncomfortable kinship and wield their sexuality as weapons, and, ultimately, employ disease as a form of suicide. Do they really find what it is they're looking for as the play reaches its violent and disturbing conclusion?

"... full of funny exchanges, a sharp sense of paradox and some genuine drama ... sparks fly."
> **— The New York Daily News**

"Intense ... very funny ... riveting."
> **— The New Yorker**

"UNCLE BOB moves Pendleton unequivocally into the ranks of noteworthy playwrights."
> **— Nassau Herald**

"UNCLE BOB, very Strindbergian, by the way, is about Power. Yet it still left me feeling ... dare one say the word in polite society these days? — shocked."
> **— The New York Post**

"... This is superb theater ... one stunning surprise after another, unrelenting and uncompromising to the last, Austin Pendleton's play is a triumph...."
> **— Drama-Logue**

ISBN: 0-8222-1476-8   Catalogue No.: 6099